Tales Of A Nomadic Heart

Ruthanne Cuthbert

BookLeaf
Publishing

Tales Of A Nomadic Heart © 2022
Ruthanne Cuthbert

All rights reserved.

No part of this publication may be
reproduced, stored in a retrieval system, or
transmitted, in any form or by any means,
electronic, mechanical, photocopying,
recording or otherwise, without the prior
written permission of the presenters.

Ruthanne Cuthbert asserts the moral right
to be identified as author of this work.

Presentation by *BookLeaf Publishing*

Web: www.bookleafpub.com

E-mail: info@bookleafpub.com

ISBN: 9789357210959

First edition 2022

DEDICATION

I'm dedicating this book to a few people. Who have pushed to follow my dreams. Those people are my little sister Faith, my boyfriend Daryl, his brother Shawn. Thank you guys so much for inspiring me, and giving the extra courage to take this leap of faith.

Drowning Doubts

i find myself
lying awake
battling
my darkest fear
the voices
choking me
whispers
won't let me go
i can't hear
anything else
all these lies
choking me
is the only sound
i can hear
now

A Troubled Heart

sitting here
thinking
with an empty heart
just thinking
where did i go wrong?
is there a way to fix this?

do i just...
walk away
or stay here
what should i do

To Those Who Have Scaficed All

as i look around
i can see the people whom
have come before us
the names of those people
they giving all that they could
for us and the generations to come
their legacy leaving an imprint on us
and those to come after
many have given there lives to us
for us

we stand silently saluting them
for what they have given up for us
to give us the chance to keep living
that we take all too much for grant it
forgetting what it has cost us all
and still costs us as people stand
protecting our lives
people have fallen and still fall
giving everything for us
they stand one last time; protecting

silently; standing saluting
vigilantly watching

the flag raises in honor
of those who fallen
the flag raises in honor
of those who have fallen
they honor those
who gave all
on the emergency
the cost was high
now we come back
to honor that cost

A Last Pleading Promise

locked up inside
calling out my name
i can feel you
i'm tempted to follow you
cut will i fade if i follow
i'm much to young to face you
to know your empty promises
torn apart with pain
your afflictions breaking me

sell me your promises; turning away
stripping me away destroying
now i see the fire
letting me fall away
you build me up just to let me slip
down this spiraling dark hole
incomplete i run away

A Lovely Day Dream

i never thought
i would see the day
that things would fall into place
almost hard to believe
so i hold my breath
wondering will this actually
last...
or am i just day dreaming

Uniquely You

what makes a person
who they are
their differences
no matter
how small
or big they are
though
some would believe
that gives
a rite
to judge
others not so
if a judgment
is to be made
you must have
walked in their shoes
if only that was possible
maybe people
would see
in a new light
that
though you may be different
you're still alike
in so many ways
see the differences

are something the best parts
of who we are

The Cursed Blessing

to be alone
is a curse and blessing
all in one
one for no one
what's it like
to not be
i have no clue
i wish
i knew
what it was

Is This The Last Time...

they send me away
to find me a way my hearts slipping
away
locked inside
these secrets
i can't find an escape
a dangerous shadow follows me
its sings in my head
dangerous thoughts
it begs me to follow
i'm walking by myself
but i'm not myself
beside myself
echoes nothingness
every scream never gets out

My Promise

promising
to never leave
i stay here
with you
i'm yours
till the day i die
that is my promise
to you

To Let Go

the past is not a place you should dwell in
all that will come from it
is chewing you up and spitting you out
malice and spitefullness
are not the path that should be taken
envy, jealousy, malice, spite
you should not just use to bring chaos
upon others
the emotions of others
are not one your right or place
to toy with
leave it be and let go
nothing good will come of chaos
choose not the dark but the light
be the flame burning brightly
in the sky
swim deep inside
the sea is full of wonders

Better Days Are Promised

let the past go take a deep breath
past the sunrise ahead
there is always yet another beautiful day to
breath life into
within all the chaos
past the tears rushing down
the walls tumbling down
to pieces

there is always
a quiet to the storm
raging inside you

hush hush little one the storm
will soon end
and die down inside
all will be well enough soon

the infinity of time
heals all
soon the same will be felt by you

letting go
i know it's very hard
truly inside you know

happiness
comes in many forms
sometimes not easily seen
but always felt

Comparative Times Now

Does it ever work that way?
Can you read it all the time
Through and through
No it doesn't
Never should have felt this way
I knew better from the start
But then I never would have known
Just what we were
I don't want to let it go
But you already knew that
Didn't you?

That's why you pulled me in
The innocence charmed you
That you wanted to keep for yourself
The foolishness of youth
I wish I never knew

Is This The Beginning Of The End

Aren't you alive?
Maybe not
Just breathing

Then why only just breathe
Why not be living
Look inside
Find all you believe
Don't try to prove
Anything
To no one
You owe nothing
Only owe yourself
To be who your meant to be
Can you succeed
Atleast that

Thoughts Of A Healing Mind

Every day I wake up
Is this nightmare still
My reality
The opinions and lectures
Only meant to oppress us
Maybe that ignorance is a bliss
Only is it really?
The walls we put up meant to protect us
But they only show us limitations
Can we provide a better answer
Not just hiding in fear
Show the truth
Nothing is gained in deceit
Or else it just becomes an
Endless loop
Of just searching for a purpose
Trying to hide from the turbulence
Except you can't you just
Got to get through it all
Yet you feel like taking off
Sometimes maybe life is just a nuisance
In your in own mind

Through The Eyes Of Sadness

I used to hate me
I couldn't face a mirror
Me or the mirror
    Without wanting to break
I'm not positive of
Tearing up from the inside
Out
I never would have thought
I could face me or the outside world

Yet here I am now
More positive than ever before
I never would have known before
That I could become this
It's so beautiful
Finally being able to see me

For who I am
Truly
So many fears
I had to overcome
To come to this point
In our world today
I been through

So many changes

Do I give a damn
No it's just tough luck
With my face in my plams
I want to take off
Sometimes all I feel
Is lost
Is it controlling you
The pain of all the losses

Never is pain permanent
Just gotta get through this
Can you reverse it?
But is it worth it?
Promise me you will get through this
I know such a nusiance
Life feels like
Just going through motions

Engulfed Perspectives

Did you know that perception
Is the most important trait
One can learn
Not all accomplish this
Never changing their closed eyes
They faulture so far away
From the truth

Has that become you?
Has the turbulence of society
Swept you away off your feet
Clouding all
Can you pull the veil off your eyes
To find the solution

Erase the fog from your mind
To become wiser than you
Have ever known
Can you be this?

Unlearn society`s failed perspective
So you can accept all
With arms wide open
Becoming them to teach

You more
Each experience
All has is yes unique
In its self
Still there is so much
One can learn from others
Only if they choose to listen
Though

What will your descion be?

Critiquting One's Self

All the things I've got bottled up
Are starting to take there toll finally
I'm not sure who I am anymore
It's useless to try and make it all go away
At the end of it all
The disappointment inflicted on myself
This time I might just say goodbye
For a while

Don't come looking for me
Trust me I'm alright just recovering
Trying to recognize myself
In the person I see
In the mirror reflecting back at me
If I stare hard enough maybe
I can see me

Where did the emotion go
In my eyes
Such a fleeting stare
Runaway; runaway
They say pleading
Begging for someone to see
Inside through the walls put up
Past the pain

Finding the greater purpose for you
Only if you will believe
You deserve as much

From The Beginning Wondering Is This Only The Beginning

Too many changes are happening
Is there anywhere near the truth
Im not sure if I just missed it all
I never really have understood
What an argument or what a start is

Is there a way through the racing game
Am I at the start line or even near there
Is this realirealistic or worse
Not a reality but just a dream
What is communication
Is this a possibility
Have we blew it all already
Is there any confidence
To come from the past
To bring forward

Can barely find the answer
Away from all this
I don't know a home
But I will pursue this purpose
For a belonging

A home
Do you know the consequence
Of not belonging
I promise you will regret it
The safety you can't recover
Or recognize

The fights can't compete
Or will you compete with the fights
Raging inside
I never received the confirmation
For where to go from here

Lost In Broken Times

The past...
I let go
It doesn't change
It happened

Now
It's gone
Where did it go
So wrong

Now it falls away
The accusations
The lies
The betrayal

Maybe you don't see it
I do though
You look at me differently

I have lost all
My friend...
Everything

Somewhere
I went wrong...
Along this path

Wherever Has it Gone

Looking for that sign
I have no clue
If i can be what
I hope to be
Always in my mind

I feel
I can't keep the track
Of the time
Anymore
Can I find something
I love
And just build
My own way

I miss the times
When the cares of the world
Didn't need to be a worry
Weren't even a thought on your mind
What happened
In the space between then
And now
Never would have thought
So much could
Change

I can't waste anytime though
Reliving the moments of the past
Will only give it power
To haunt you
Weather your asleep or awake
You won't even notice
It consciously poison
Your mind
You'll look a blind eye
As it seeps to your core
Begging to drop you to your knees

Time To Live And Time To Die

If I fall asleep
I see a new tomorrow
But do i want to see
A new tomorrow

I need to block the noise
A moment silence
Is all I need

When I'm fucked up
I feel safer
When I'm sober
I can't compete
With the demons
Racing inside of me
Reflection on this position
I've taken a place
At the stand
I shouldn't
Do this again

Been going through
The motions
I can barely find myself

Where has the time gone
The days
I took for granted
Oh I wish
How I could those back
Been through so many changes
Can I even look through a mirror
And see myself

It's not just easy to change
You can't just flip it like a switch
To turn off the past
It's a part of who I am

That's why I never fit
In the puzzle left of life
But I prefer to be outside the box
Rather than fit perfectly in that box

They try to lock us
In place
I would rather travel see
All there is to see

The evil
Travel to the rock bottom
Be with the lowest of low
Then at least

I can attest
To having understanding

When your on your knees
Begging for it end
Thinking your going crazy
Yea you have a lot of shit to work on
Running to nowhere it feels like
You see right through
All the bullshit

Falling asleep with all the demons
I see them in my asleep
And even my flashbacks
I can't just push down
The past like that
I know it puts resistants
On my mind
I can't tell no one
It's hidden right underneath the surface
It's so hard to word it sometimes

The amount of long nights out number
The good nights
But what the fuck am I supposed do
You think

Then eyes open wide
Judgment fades away

The more experience
You have
 Then comes wisdom
 With the ability
 To communicate
With all

Then you can make a sound
When you come back up
Swinging
With a new purpose
And perspective of life
New meaning

www.ingramcontent.com/pod-product-compliance
Lightning Source LLC
La Vergne TN
LVHW051244200726
843510LV00011B/1682